Sports Illustrated KID$

STARS OF SPORTS

SIMONE BILES

GYMNASTICS LEGEND

by Lisa M. Bolt Simons

CAPSTONE PRESS
a capstone imprint

Stars of Sports is published by Capstone Press, an imprint of Capstone.
1710 Roe Crest Drive,
North Mankato, Minnesota 56003
www.capstonepub.com

Library of Congress Cataloging-in-Publication Data
Names: Simons, Lisa M. B., 1969– author.
Title: Simone Biles : gymnastics legend / by Lisa M. Bolt Simons.
Description: North Mankato, Minnesota : Capstone Press, a Capstone imprint, [2021] |
   Series: Sports illustrated kids stars of sports | Includes bibliographical references and index. |
   Audience: Ages 8–11 | Audience: Grades 4–6
Identifiers: LCCN 2020037776 (print) | LCCN 2020037777 (ebook) | ISBN 9781496695253
   (hardcover) | ISBN 9781977154897 (ebook PDF) | ISBN 9781977156556 (kindle edition)
Subjects: LCSH: Biles, Simone, 1997– —Juvenile literature. | Gymnasts—United States—
   Biography—Juvenile literature. | Women gymnasts—United States—Biography—Juvenile literature.
Classification: LCC GV460.2.B55 B65 2021 (print) | LCC GV460.2.B55 (ebook) |
   DDC 796.44092 [B]—dc23
LC record available at https://lccn.loc.gov/2020037776
LC ebook record available at https://lccn.loc.gov/2020037777

Summary: Simone Biles may be small in size, but she is larger than life in the sport of gymnastics!
A coach recognized Biles's natural talent at just six years old. Since then, Biles has overcome many
challenges to become the most successful gymnast of all time. Find out how she worked her way to
the top of the Olympic podium and learn what she plans to do next.

Editorial Credits
Mandy Robbins, editor; Heidi Thompson, designer; Eric Gohl, media researcher;
Spencer Rosio, production specialist

Photo Credits
AP Images : David J. Phillip, 27, Virginia Mayo, 15; Getty Images: Bob Levey, 26, JOHN THYS, 5,
Maddie Meyer, 8, Tim Clayton/Corbis, 12, 13; Newscom: Amy Sanderson/ZUMA Press, 21, Li Qiaoqiao
Xinhua News Agency, 19, MIKE BLAKE/REUTERS, 7, Mike Theiler/UPI Photo, 17, picture alliance/
Sven Simon/Frank Hoermann, Cover, Thomas Eisenhuth/dpa/picture-alliance, 11; Shutterstock:
A.RICARDO, 23, Alex Kravtsov, 1; Sports Illustrated: Erick W. Rasco, 28, Robert Beck, 25

All internet sites appearing in back matter were available and accurate when this book was sent to press.

Direct Quotations
Page 4: from "Frame by Frame, Moves That Made Simone Biles Unbeatable," *New York Times,* August
   11, 2016, https://www.nytimes.com/interactive/2016/08/11/sports/olympics/simone-biles-winning-
   moves.html?mtrref=undefined&assetType=REGIWALL&mtrref=undefined&assetType=REGIWALL.
Page 13: from "Gold Rush," by Michael Hardy, *Texas Monthly*, July 2016,
   https://www.texasmonthly.com/the-culture/simone-biles-olympic-gymnast/
Page 15: from "Simone Biles Crowned Gymnastics All-Around World Champion," *Associated Press*,
   October 4, 2013, https://www.teamusa.org/News/2013/October/04/Simone-Biles-Crowned-
   Gymnastics-All-Around-World-Champion.
Page 19: from "Team USA Women's Gymnasts Golden at World Championships," by Amy Rosewater,
   October 8, 2014, https://www.teamusa.org/News/2014/October/08/Team-USA-Womens-Gymnasts-
   Golden-At-World-Championships.
Page 22: from "Gymnast Simone Biles Teams Up with Mattress Firm for Philanthropic Efforts," by Tony
   Cantu, *Patch*, September 22, 2016, https://patch.com/us/across-america/gymnast-simone-biles-teams-
   mattress-firm-philanthropic-efforts.
Page 24: from *Courage to Soar: a Body in Motion, A Life in Balance* by Simone Biles and Michelle
   Burford. Grand Rapids, MI: Zondervan, 2016.
Page 27: from "Simone Biles Opens Up About How She Coped with Sexual Abuse," interview with
   Priyanka Chopra, March 29, 2019, https://www.youtube.com/watch?v=dk_9IiizZlQ.

TABLE OF CONTENTS

Glossary terms are **BOLD** on first use.

THE "BILES"

The 2013 World Artistic Gymnastics Championships took place in Antwerp, Belgium. Promising young gymnast Simone Biles was on the floor. When the music started, she dazzled the audience with a near-perfect routine. Biles not only had complex moves across the floor, but she had also created a signature move—the "Biles."

She started with a back **handspring**. Then she went into a double **layout** with a half-turn. The move ended with a **blind landing**. The audience went wild! Her stunning performance helped her win gold to become the All-Around World Champion gymnast.

"My coach was like, well, what if you do a half-turn?" Biles said after the 2013 World Championships. "Then you could get it named after you if you competed at a world event."

At just 16 years old, Biles was already a world champion gymnast. But she was just getting started.

CHAPTER ONE
A DIFFICULT START

Simone Arianne Biles was born on March 14, 1997, in Columbus, Ohio. She and her three siblings were put in **foster care**.

When she was six years old, Biles's grandparents adopted her and her younger sister, Adria. They went to live with their grandparents near Houston, Texas. Another family member adopted her older siblings, Tevin and Ashley. Simone and Adria called their grandparents Mom and Dad. Their uncles, Ron and Adam, became their adopted brothers.

From day one, Biles was always moving. She liked to do somersaults and backflips. She especially loved the trampoline.

〈〈〈 Biles's parents cheer her on at the 2016 Summer Olympics in Rio De Janeiro, Brazil.

One day Biles's daycare took a field trip to Bannon's Gymnastix center. Biles watched the gymnasts. She tried to copy their moves. Her brother Adam challenged her to do a backflip. She did two!

A STRONG COMPETITOR

One of the coaches at the gym gave Adam a letter for Biles's parents. It invited her to join Bannon's Gymnastix.

<<< Biles trained with coach Aimee Boorman at Bannon's Gymnastix.

Biles wanted to learn all about gymnastics. She was finally getting training for the tumbling, flipping, and somersaulting she loved to do. Biles quickly picked up all four events—the floor, the vault, the uneven bars, and the balance beam. In gymnastics, the all-around competition includes all four events, with the four scores added together.

Biles was a natural. She soon started competing in club **meets**. They led to local, state, and **regional** meets. Biles became a strong competitor. It didn't take long for her to reach the national level. Her first national meet was in Houston, Texas, at the 2011 American Classic. She won third in the all-around and first place in vault!

FACT

Biles is 4 feet, 8 inches (142 centimeters) tall. The average height of female gymnasts is 5 feet, 1 inch (155 cm).

CHAPTER TWO
MEDALS AND MISERY

In 2011, Biles qualified for the American Classic tournament at the Károlyi Ranch in Texas. The ranch was owned by Martha and Bela Károlyi, legendary gymnastics coaches. If Biles impressed them, she could train with **elite** gymnasts. These were the same young women who competed to be on the U.S. Olympic team.

Martha Károlyi saw that Biles had what it took to be a star gymnast. She invited Biles to train monthly with the national team. They had 28 junior and senior gymnasts from across the United States.

FACT

The U.S. national team usually has 16 senior gymnasts. Only the best are chosen to go to the Olympics for Team USA. The highest number of gymnasts picked for Team USA has been seven. There are usually a few alternates as well.

In 2013, at age 16, Biles was officially named to the senior national team. Meets now included international competitions. Biles represented the USA. Biles won several gold medals in Italy and Germany.

⟨⟨⟨ Biles performs a balancing move on the beam at a 2013 competition in Germany.

MENTAL TOUGHNESS

Four months later, Biles was in Chicago, Illinois, at the Secret U.S. Classic. This meet showcased only elite U.S. gymnasts. It was the last meet before nationals. But Biles wasn't doing well.

First, Biles fell from the uneven bars. Then, she slipped on the balance beam. During the floor exercise, she hurt her ankle. She couldn't compete on the vault. Biles came in thirteenth at the meet. She was frustrated and upset.

>>> Biles wows the audience with her beam routine at the 2013 P&G Championship.

"I felt like my life was going down the drain," she said.

Biles started meeting with a sports **psychology** coach named Robert Andrews. The counseling sessions helped. The next month, Biles competed at the P&G Championships in Connecticut. She took silver in the four individual events. She was named the national champion in the all-around!

⟨⟨⟨ Biles stands on the podium with Kyla Ross (left) and Brenna Dowell (right) after winning the 2013 P&G Championship.

HITTING HER STRIDE

Biles's next big international competition was the 2013 World Artistic Gymnastics Championships in Belgium. The event would be tough. It was Biles's first time competing there, and she would be up against world champions and Olympians. Would she be ready both physically and mentally? Would the counseling sessions with Andrews still help?

Biles led by just 0.016 points going into the floor event. But her routine included more difficult moves than she had ever done before. Biles made them look easy.

Award-Winning History

Biles was the first Black woman to win an all-around World Championship. But others helped pave the way. Luci Collins was the first Black gymnast to make a U.S. Olympic team in 1980. Dominique Dawes was the first to win Olympic gold in 1996. Gabby Douglas was the first to win gold in the individual all-around in the 2016 Olympics. Now Biles is making even more history!

〉〉〉 Biles performs her impressive floor routine at the 2013 World Artistic Gymnastics Championships.

"On floor, I just have a lot of fun," Biles said. "That is the main key."

Biles won a gold medal in the floor event! She won a silver medal for the vault and bronze for the balance beam. On the uneven bars, Biles got fourth. Then she won another gold medal for the all-around event. Biles was a world champion!

CHAPTER THREE
INJURY AND RECOVERY

In October 2013, Biles had surgery. Doctors removed a bone spur in her leg. A bone spur is a tiny, pointed piece of bone that sticks out from other bones. After surgery, Biles couldn't practice for three weeks. She needed to heal. But healing took time away from training.

Then in March 2014, Biles's shoulder started to bother her. Her coach thought it was from training too hard. This time, Biles tried **rehabilitation** instead of surgery. She missed the 2014 AT&T American Cup. Then she withdrew before another meet.

Biles's injuries frustrated her. She wanted to return to competition as soon as she could. Each event prepares gymnasts for the next one. These events lead to the national competition. Nationals lead to the World Championships. And then come the Olympics, which are held every four years. In 2014, the next Olympics were just two years away.

FACT

In a 2013 podcast, Biles said her gymnastic idols were Shawn Johnson and Aly Raisman.

〉〉〉 Shawn Johnson won a total of 16 medals during her gymnastics career.

THE COMEBACK QUEEN

In August 2014, Biles returned to the Secret U.S. Classic. Her shoulder was healthy again, and her confidence was back. Biles won three individual golds and one all-around gold!

The same month, she competed in the P&G Gymnastics Championships. She got fourth on the uneven bars. She tied for second on the balance beam. But the highlight was Biles's floor routine. She performed it perfectly, defending her title as champion with a high score of 122.550 points!

Sidesteppin' Simone

Biles is famous for her flips and twists. But how fast can she sidestep? Scared of bugs, Biles got chased by a bee after winning her second World Championship in China. The bee was on her bouquet of flowers. Biles jumped off the podium to avoid the bee. Then she quickly sidestepped and jumped on the podium with the silver medalist! The bee eventually flew away. The video has been watched more than three million times on YouTube.

In September 2014, the World Championships were held in Nanning, China. Biles won silver on the vault. She performed a difficult move called an Amanar. Biles won gold on the beam, even after a stumble.

"We had a couple mistakes. . . . yeah, me, I did, but other than that, we did pretty good," she said.

Her team won gold. Biles's floor routine included impressive tumbling passes. She won gold for the all-around. Biles defended her title!

⟨⟨⟨ Biles performs her floor routine at the 2014 World Championships with her signature smile.

CHAPTER FOUR

MAKING HISTORY

In 2015, Biles was ready to take her gymnastics career to the next level. It began at the World Championships in Glasgow, Scotland. Biles won a bronze for vault. She won gold in the team competition, floor, and balance beam.

Things got rough during the all-around competition. Biles over-rotated a front flip on the balance beam. She grabbed the beam so she wouldn't fall. During her floor routine, she stepped out of bounds, losing 0.3 points. Despite these mistakes, Biles won the all-around title by more than a full point. She was the first woman to win three world titles in a row!

FACT

Biles was the first woman to win three world titles in a row but not the first to win three world titles. Russian legend Svetlana Korkhina did so in 1997, 2001, and 2003.

⟨⟨⟨ Biles seems to defy gravity during her floor
routine at the 2015 World Championships.

With 14 World Championship medals, Biles
became the most successful American gymnast of all
time. She also had a record 10 World Championship
titles—the first female gymnast to earn that many.

GOING PRO

Biles was on fire! In the summer of 2015, she made a big decision. Biles decided to turn professional. She had planned to attend college at the University of California, Los Angeles. But her dad said she could still go to college one day. She couldn't always turn pro.

Going pro meant **sponsors** paid Biles a lot of money. She had to wear their company clothes and star in their commercials. The Olympics were the next year. Her sponsors started to showcase Biles on Team USA.

Fostering Support

Outside the gym, Biles supports programs that focus on the needs of foster children. She always shares her story of growing up in foster care. She has focused on helping foster children get the sleep they need in what can be a stressful situation. Biles has also volunteered and helped with getting donations for foster-care organizations. "Children are children; they need our love, support and help to understand the benefits of sleep and the role it plays in an active and healthy life," she said.

⟨⟨⟨ Biles practices with her Team USA teammates
for the 2016 Olympics.

In December, Biles got another award for her
gymnastics skills, but it wasn't a medal. The U.S.
Olympic Committee named her Female Olympic
Athlete of the Year.

CHAPTER FIVE

THE OLYMPICS

The 2016 Olympic Games were held in Rio de Janeiro, Brazil. Biles was on a team with four other gymnasts. They were Gabby Douglas, Laurie Hernandez, Madison Kocian, and Aly Raisman. The women were called "The Final Five" because it would be coach Martha Károlyi's last year coaching at the Olympics.

Biles helped Team USA win the gold medal. She also earned a gold medal for the vault and the individual all-around. But then Biles stumbled on the balance beam. Because of this, she got a bronze medal. But she came back on the floor exercise and earned her fourth Olympic gold!

Of her Olympic success, Biles said, "No one is more surprised than I am that the little girl with the big muscles ended up on a path from foster care to an Olympic stadium in Rio de Janiero, Brazil."

⟨⟨⟨ Biles waves to the crowd after her stunning 2016 Olympic floor routine.

OVERCOMING ABUSE

In January 2018, Biles faced a different challenge. USA Gymnastics team doctor Larry Nassar was on trial for abuse. He had hurt a lot of gymnasts in secret for years. Biles and her teammates were among them.

At first, Biles didn't want to talk about what had happened. But the less she spoke about it, the more troubled she became. Biles finally decided to go to therapy. As she grew stronger, she began to share her story.

⟨⟨⟨ Biles poses with a young fan.

<<< Biles speaks to young gymnasts at the Károlyi Ranch.

"It wasn't easy, but I feel like I'm a stronger woman today, and I feel like telling my story has helped younger girls," she said.

Biles moved forward with her life the only way she knew how—by competing. At the 2019 World Championships in Stuttgart, Germany, Biles won five more gold medals. With 25 medals, she had become the most successful gymnast in the world!

WHAT'S NEXT?

Biles next eyed the 2020 Olympics in Tokyo, Japan. But because of the coronavirus **pandemic**, the Olympics were postponed.

When Biles first found out, she cried. But she knew people needed to be safe and healthy.

Biles is committed to staying fit. She has at-home workouts. Biles believes in staying fit mentally too. She goes to therapy and surrounds herself with people she loves. When the Olympics are rescheduled, she'll be ready to make history yet again!

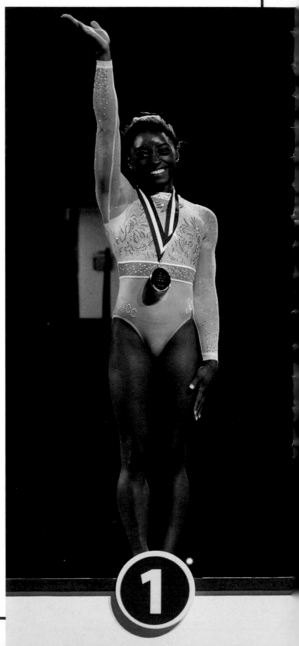

〉〉〉 Biles won the gold at the 2018 U.S. National Championships.

TIMELINE

1997 Simone Biles is born in Columbus, Ohio.

2011 Biles begins her junior elite career.

2013 Biles is named to the senior national team at age 16.

2013 Biles introduces the "Biles," a double layout with a half turn, at the World Championships in Belgium. With it, she wins her first World Championship.

2014 Biles is named Sportswoman of the Year by the Women's Sports Foundation.

2015 Biles turns professional and wins her third straight all-around title at the World Championships in Glasgow, Scotland.

2016 Biles wins four gold medals and one bronze at the Olympics in Rio de Janeiro, Brazil, to become the first U.S. female gymnast to win four golds at an Olympics.

2017 Biles is named the Best Female Athlete at the 2017 ESPY Awards and Laureus World Sportswoman of the Year.

2018 Biles introduces a vault element named the "Biles" at the World Championships in Qatar.

2018 Biles is named ESPN Magazine's Most Dominant Athlete of 2018.

2019 Biles wins the World Championship for the fifth time. She wins five gold medals, bringing her medal total to 25, 19 of which are golds.

GLOSSARY

BLIND LANDING (BLYND LAND-ing)—when a gymnast performs a skill and doesn't see the ground before he or she lands

ELITE (ih-LEET)—the best of anything or the highest class

FOSTER CARE (FAWS-tuhr KARE)—a system in which children are placed in a safe home for a short time if they are unable to live with their parents

HANDSPRING (HAND-spring)—when a person starts in a standing position and turns the body in a full circle, landing on the hands and then the feet

LAYOUT (LAY-out)—a rotating skill in which the athlete's body is almost straight

MEET (MEET)—a sporting event featuring many contests

PANDEMIC (pan-DEM-ic)—an illness spread over an entire country, continent, or the world that affects millions of people

PSYCHOLOGY (sye-KOH-luh-jee)—the study of the mind, the emotions, and human behavior

REGIONAL (REE-juh-nuhl)—of or relating to a local part of a larger area

REHABILITATION (ree-huh-bil-uh-TAY-shun)—therapy that helps people recover their health or abilities

SPONSOR (SPON-sur)—a company that pays an athlete in exchange for helping the business advertise its products

READ MORE

Abdo, Kenny. *Simone Biles*. Minneapolis: Abdo Publishing, 2020.

Burns, Kylie. *Simone Biles: Gold Medal Gymnast and Advocate for Healthy Living*. New York: Crabtree Publishing Company, 2018.

Fishman, Jon. *Gymnastics Superstar Simone Biles*. Minneapolis: Lerner Publishing Group, 2019.

INTERNET SITES

Simone Biles
simonebiles.com/

Simone Biles
olympic.org/simone-biles

Simone Biles
usagym.org/pages/athletes/athleteListDetail.html?id=164887

INDEX